MW01134644

SMALL TALK
HACKS

*The People and Communication Skills You Need to Talk to Anyone
& Be Instantly Likeable*

Akash P. Karia
#1 Internationally Bestselling Author of
"CHARISMA: 34 Little Tricks to Unlock Your Inner
Charisma" and
"How Successful People Think Differently"
www.AkashKaria.com

BESTSELLING BOOKS BY AKASH KARIA

Available on Amazon (www.bit.ly/AkashKaria):

CHARISMA: 34 Little Tricks to Unlock Your Inner Charisma

How to Deliver a Great TED Talk

How to Design TED-Worthy Presentation Slides

Own the Room: Presentation Techniques to Keep Your Audience on the Edge of Their Seats

ANTI Negativity: How to Stop Negative Thinking and Lead a Positive Life

Persuasion Psychology: 26 Powerful Techniques to Persuade Anyone!

How Successful People Think Differently

FREE RESOURCES

There are hundreds of free articles as well as several eBooks, MP3s and videos on Akash's blog. To get instant access to those, head over to www.AkashKaria.com.

RAVE REVIEWS FOR "SMALL TALK HACKS"

"Akash Karia is a communications expert. He has the people skills to go with it. This book is easy to read and packed with tips and techniques that you can implement immediately.

This isn't just about talking. Akash covers non-verbal cues, questioning and listening techniques as well as how to improve your charisma. He then steps it up a notch and tells you how leverage these techniques and take it to the next level.

It doesn't matter if you're an introvert or an extrovert, a confident talker or not, this book will have takeaways for everyone."
~ Alastair Macartney, BASE Jumping World Champion & Bestselling Author of Perfect Madness

"I really enjoyed this book! The best part is the "Try This" suggestions after the different techniques that are explained in detail. [Small Talk Hacks] is great for introverts or anyone looking to calm the nerves in social situations. The tips are easy to remember and practice."
~ Harlan Yee
"Really interesting book [with] lots of research studies quoted [and] simple actionable advice."
~ Pedro Ruao

CONTENTS

Chapter 1   Creating A Stellar First Impression With
             Non-Verbal Communication   1

Chapter 2   Breaking Through Fear
             And Breaking The Ice   15

Chapter 3   How To Seal A Memorable Verbal
             Impression In 30 Seconds   29

Chapter 4   How To Become An Active Listener   37

Chapter 5   How To Make Your Personality Shine   51

Chapter 6   Going From Introduction To Intimacy   59

Chapter 7   How To Keep Your Conversation Alive   75

Chapter 8   How To Avoid Stopping A
             Conversation Cold   81

Chapter 9   How To End The Conversation Positively   89

Chapter 10   Following Up On A Conversation To Deepen
               The Relationship   95

Chapter 11   Wrap Up   101

               Questions Or Comments?   111

               You Might Also Enjoy   113

               About The Author   116

YOUR FREE GIFT

As a way of saying thank you for your purchase, I'd like to offer you a free bonus package worth $297. This bonus package contains eBooks, videos and audiotapes on how master the art of persuasion, become a great public speaker and develop your charisma. You can download the free bonus here:

www.AkashKaria.com/FREE

For Chloe Sha,
Because I love how we can talk for hours
And not say anything at all,
But know that we had a good time saying it.

Chapter 1

CREATING A STELLAR FIRST IMPRESSION WITH NON-VERBAL COMMUNICATION

How quickly do you make judgments about people?

We'd like to think that we don't judge people until we get to know them. But the truth is it only takes a tenth of a second to make an accurate judgment about someone you meet or see.

Research shows that this is true. In 2005, a study conducted by Alex Todorov, a psychologist at Princeton University, along with his student research assistant Janine Willis, proved this. During the study, participants were asked to watch a short video – less than a second – of political candidates. They were then asked to predict who would win the election. What's so interesting is that with just that tiny exposure to video, the participants made correct predictions 70% of the time.

What does that mean? It means that most of us make instant judgments that have a real impact over time.

As a speaker, you need to be able to create a great first impression – within a tenth of a second. How do you do that? I have five surefire techniques that will help you to do just that.

TECHNIQUE #1: MAKE A CONSCIOUS CHOICE TO BE ENTHUSIASTIC

Whether you realize it or not, people can immediately pick up on your energy. When you go into any type of interaction – a job interview or even a social party – people will quickly know how you're feeling internally.

If you feel nervous, that energy will permeate the room and everyone will know it. If you feel angry, you can turn people off immediately as they sense your negative energy. Even if you try to mask it, you'll be sending out energy waves that can't be hidden.

This is one way that people develop a gut feeling about you – they pick up on your energy. And most people are very good at picking up on this whether they know it or not. That makes it important for you to go into any interaction by setting the right intention beforehand.

So, what is the right intention?

As an introvert myself, I've found that the best way to approach any interaction and achieve maximum success is to do it with ENTHUSIASM. That means making a conscious decision to be enthusiastic instead of anxious.

But can you really control your energy that well?

In fact, it is possible to create feelings of happiness and enthusiasm. Two different studies conducted by Yuna L. Ferguson, a researcher at Knox College, and Kennon M. Sheldon, a researcher at the University of Missouri, found that it's possible to change your own mood.

Researchers asked two groups of participants to listen to music that is considered "happy." One group was told to try to avoid relaxing and improving their moods while the other group was told to consciously work toward feeling happier. Other groups were asked to do the same thing without the happy music.

In the end, the group that was the happiest was the one that both listened to happy music and focused on trying to feel happy as well.

What that means for you is that you can make a conscious decision to be happy and you can also make a conscious decision to be enthusiastic. We have much more control over our emotions and energy than you might think!

What's the reward for going into an interaction with enthusiasm? People will see you as open and positive and they'll respond well to you. But when you lead with nervous and anxious energy, you tend to close yourself off to others.

So here's what I encourage you to do: Make a conscious decision to be enthusiastic. By doing so, your body language will naturally mirror that emotion. You'll exude positive, friendly, and warm energy that will draw people to you and help them to see you in a positive light.

Try This:
Before you go to your next social gathering, make a conscious decision to be enthusiastic. It will help to think of the excitement of making new friends or the taste of the delicious party food (you can focus on anything positive about the event).

You might even want to try snapping your fingers to "snap" yourself out of anxiety. This helps to break up nervous energy and allows you to refocus on becoming enthusiastic instead.

Exercise is another way to help use up nervous energy and promote a more relaxed, but enthusiastic energy. Before a big event try going for a ten-minute walk or jog – or even do a few jumping jacks.

TECHNIQUE #2: BE AWARE OF YOUR POSTURE

How you hold yourself says a lot about how you feel – even though this may be an unconscious message. What is your body language saying about you?

When you're preparing to go into any interaction, it's important to be aware of your body language and make sure that it's sending the message you want it to send.

Take a moment and write down the characteristics you want people to associate with you as soon as they see you. Write down at least five characteristics. Some examples include:

- confident
- open
- enthusiastic
- bold
- strong
- comfortable in your own skin

Next, I want you to think of someone who embodies these characteristics. Who comes to mind?

Once you have a particular person in your mind, visualize him or her. How does he or she stand? What do you notice about his or her movement? What type of posture are you envisioning?

Now, take on that same posture. Are your shoulders pointed up or slumped down? Is your back straight or bent over? Notice all the adjustments you have to make in order to exhibit the same posture.

Once you've achieved a similar posture, pay attention to how it feels. This is the posture that you want to have when you go into any interaction.

According to social psychologist and Harvard faculty member Amy Cuddy, your body language not only affects how people see you but also how you see yourself. Her research (www.AkashKaria.com/Amy) has shown that when you stand in a high-confidence posture, your confidence levels also increase.

At the same time, when you're standing confidently with your shoulders back, spine straight, chest out, and feet planted firmly shoulder-width apart, you also have a decrease in the levels of the hormone cortisol.

Cortisol is a hormone produced when you're experiencing stress. So simply standing confidently actually reduces your physical stress levels. The inverse is also true. When you stand in a low-confidence posture with your head down and shoulders slumped forward, your cortisol level actually increases.

This is very powerful research. It reveals that body language actually has an effect not only in the way people perceive you but also in your physical stress levels and the way you see yourself.

Try This:
Before going to your next event, stand in a high-confidence posture for at least two minutes. Your head should be held high, your shoulders back, and your chest out. Remember to emulate the posture of the confident person you admire and carry yourself that way the entire time. For more power poses, watch Amy's TED talk on www.AkashKaria.com/Amy.

TECHNIQUE #3: SMILE
When you're in a positive mood, people will naturally be attracted to you. People love being around someone who puts them in a good mood, too.

What's the quickest way to help others feel positive?

Simple. It's to make them smile. And how do you do that? All you have to do is smile at them. In fact, a British research study found that providing one smile to another person can make them feel as good as the stimulation that would come from eating 2,000 chocolate bars at once – only without the stomachache or weight gain!

A couple of studies from Uppsala University in Sweden also bring this point home. Studies conducted in both 2002 and 2011 show that when someone smiles at you, you actually let

AKASH KARIA

go of the control you normally have on the muscles in your face.

In other words, you feel compelled to smile when someone smiles at you. Furthermore, the research shows that when someone is smiling at you it's very difficult to frown. Scientists hypothesize that smiling is contagious because it's good for the evolution of the human species.

The same thing happens over and over again, even if you're looking at a stranger that you never plan to see again.

Given that you've already made a conscious decision to be enthusiastic, smiling shouldn't be that difficult. When you smile, the whole world smiles with you!

Try This:
The next time you go to a social or business function, test this theory out. Walk up to someone you don't know, give your best smile, and introduce yourself. Watch to see how the person reacts – it's almost a given that he or she will return your smile.

TECHNIQUE #4: EYE CONTACT
One of the most important ways that we connect with people socially is through eye contact. And eye contact itself can give many different impressions. Some eye contact can be aggressive while other forms of it are welcoming.

If you are looking for an example of someone who has mastered the power of eye contact, then look no further than Bill Clinton. Here's a short description of the magical effect Clinton's eye contact had on others (via PsyBlog):

> The stories of Bill Clinton's charisma are legend.
>
> Much of that charisma was communicated through eye contact.
>
> Those who have met him say that when he looks at you, it's a very intimate experience. His eye contact is said to be deep and personal, almost mesmerising; it's as though there are only two people in the room: him and you.
>
> And he doesn't just seduce women with his eye contact, he seduces everyone.
> Clearly the eyes have enormous power, such that eye contact can have an almost magical effect on other people." – via PsyBlog (www.spring.org.uk)

Eye contact seems simple, but it can be difficult to perfect. How do you improve something that seems so automatic? And why is it so important?

Eye contact is one way that we make social connections with other people. It lets someone know that you're listening and that you're interested in them. When you give eye contact for too long, it can seem aggressive. But when you don't give enough eye contact, you can seem disinterested.

Eye contact is so powerful that it can even make people fall in love with you! A study conducted in 1989 and published by the Journal of Research in Personality found that there's a major connection between eye contact and passion.

In the study, strangers of the opposite sex were asked to gaze into each other's eyes for two minutes. In some of those interactions, that small two-minute time frame was enough for the couple to start feeling passionate feelings towards each other.

Eye contact is a large part of the process of falling in love and showing affection for one another. When you gaze into a partner's eyes, his or her body begins to produce phenylethylamine – a chemical that's associated with falling in love.

Now, our aim isn't to make people fall in love with you (I think!) – just to get them to like you. You probably won't need to gaze into someone else's eyes for two minutes. But you may want to pay attention to the way that you make eye contact.

Ask friends, colleagues, and even family members what they think about your eye contact. They may be able to tell what they think right away, or they may need a little time to observe and report back to you.

If there aren't any problems with your eye contact, you can relax. But you may get feedback about needing to have more or less eye contact. In that case, it will take some practice to make needed changes.

Try This:
If you struggle with making eye contact when you meet someone new, try turning it into a little game. Challenge yourself to pay attention to their eye color.

By focusing on the color, you'll automatically make better eye contact. Eventually this game will turn into a habit and you won't have to think about it consciously anymore.

TECHNIQUE #5: DRESS TO IMPRESS
When you're getting ready for an interaction, how much do you think about the way you dress? Whether or not you think about it, others will be quick to judge you by what you're wearing. You might be surprised by how important the way you dress really is.

In one research study, more than 300 participants were asked to look at photos of a man and a woman for three seconds. After that quick peek, they were asked to make a judgment about them.

In the case of the male photos, a man in one image was wearing a tailored suit while another man was wearing one off the rack. They were very similar in color and style, and the faces of the men in the photos were blurred so that their expressions didn't figure into the judgments.

Overall, the man who wore the tailored suit received much more favorable comments than the one in a suit off the rack.

But the interesting thing is that no one commented on his clothing at all. Instead, they commented on character traits, saying that he was more successful and more confident.

So what you wear is an expression of your character and is being judged whether you're conscious of it or not.

Does this mean you should always wear a tailored suit? Of course not! But what it does mean is that you need to put thought into what you're wearing and dress properly for every occasion. Some keys for dressing to impress include:

- Make sure your clothes fit you well – it's very inexpensive to have a tailor alter your clothing to fit you well.
- Wear high-quality fabric.
- Make sure that clothing is pressed when appropriate.
- Put effort into grooming yourself.

Doing this will help you to come across as more polished and more charismatic. You'll also feel more confident and that will put you in the right mindset to light up the room!

Try This:

Go to the tailor and get your clothes adjusted to fit you just perfectly! Clothing that you buy off the rack has been designed to fit many different body types. A tailor can take in sleeves or waistbands that are too big and give you the perfect fit.

IN A NUTSHELL

- We make judgments about people in less than a tenth of a second.
- Make a conscious choice to be enthusiastic because people unconsciously pick up on your energy levels.
- Your body language affects how you feel as well as how others perceive you. Adopt a high-confidence posture to boost your confidence levels.
- Model your posture after a charismatic, confident person that you admire.
- Smile: it's contagious and creates positive feelings between people.
- Eye contact is one of the most powerful ways of connecting with people. When you meet someone new, challenge yourself to hold eye contact long enough to notice the color of their eyes.
- People make unconscious decisions about you based on how you dress, so ensure that you're always well-groomed and wearing fitting clothes.

Chapter 2

BREAKING THROUGH FEAR AND BREAKING THE ICE

One of the hardest parts of getting to know someone new is that crucial moment when you have to break the ice. It can be incredibly difficult to walk up to a total stranger and get acquainted.

I tend to be an introvert, but I've overcome a lot of my fears by implementing the techniques I'm sharing with you in this chapter. After reading this you'll know exactly how to approach a stranger with ease and how you can move past your fears of putting yourself out there with someone new.

If you're nervous about striking up a conversation with a complete stranger, it can help to have some tried-and-true methods for breaking the ice.

TECHNIQUE #1: USE YOUR SURROUNDINGS

One of the easiest ways to broach a new conversation is to use your surroundings. After all, you're both in the same place – so that's one thing you instantly have in common!

Whether you're at a cocktail party, a conference, or a tourist location in a new city, you can use your location as a conversation starter. For example, you can ask: "Is this your first year to attend this conference? What have you liked about it so far?"

Or if you'd like to use the city you're in, you can say something like: "Are you from here?" And if they are, "What restaurants do you recommend nearby?" If they're not, you can start building a relationship by asking questions such as "Where are you from?" and "What's it like there?"

Basically you want to ask questions to engage someone about a topic that's easy and familiar. Then you can transition into a deeper conversation later if you desire.

Try This:
The next time you're at an event, learn a few facts about the event, location, or space – even write them down to help you remember them. This will give you a great jumping-off point for talking to someone new.

TECHNIQUE #2: CAPITALIZE ON CURRENT EVENTS

Before you attend any major event where you know you want to network, make sure that you spend some time catching up on current events. That can mean watching a cable news station or perusing the newspaper for a little while.

This especially works well if there's a major event in the news – it's what everyone is thinking about anyway. People love to discuss the headlines. But you want to make sure before you bring up current events that you have at least a little information about it to keep the conversation going.

Try This:

Make it a daily habit to know the major headlines going on in the world. Take a few minutes to peruse the front page of the newspaper, check out an online news site, or watch a major cable news station.

Personally, I subscribe to Business Insider's free email newsletters. The two that I enjoy most are Business Insider Select ("What you need to know every day") and Breaking News ("Get real-time alerts on major news events"). These two newsletters give me bite-sized chunks of the most important news of the day. You can sign up for free on: www.AkashKaria.com/Business

If you get in the habit of keeping updated with the happenings in your area and around the world, you'll always have something interesting to discuss.

TECHNIQUE #3: ASK GREAT QUESTIONS AND LISTEN FOR ANSWERS

How do you feel when someone asks you questions and then really takes the time to listen? For me, it feels wonderful to have someone really interested.

Asking open-ended questions is a simple way to break the ice. And then after you ask, you need to really listen to the answer you receive. A lot of people are good at asking questions, but tune out when the person answers.

> *Side note:* A close-ended question is one that limits the possible answers to "yes" and "no." An example of a close-ended question is "Did you eat?" Here, the person could answer "Yes" or "No" and that would be the end.
>
> An open-ended question, however, requires the speaker to expound and explain. An example of an open-ended question is "How was the food?" Here, the speaker has more room to talk and can say, "The chicken was delicious, but the pasta was terrible..."
>
> While close-ended questions are a natural part of a conversation, aim for more open-ended questions if

you really want to engage your partner in the conversation.

After you ask a question pause and listen for the answers. Don't spend your time trying to think of what to say next. Instead, make good eye contact and really listen to what the other person is saying.

Believe it or not, it's uncommon to come across someone who really listens, and doing this will make you both memorable and easy to talk to.

Try This:
Ask a friend to rate your listening skills. If they need some work, spend more time in your relationships trying to really listen. This will help you get into a better habit of listening that will carry over when you meet new people.

TECHNIQUE #4: JUST SAY HELLO

What's the simplest way to break the ice? It's to just say hello and introduce yourself!

You don't always need to come up with a complicated way to approach someone. Sometimes just saying, "Hello! My name is..." is enough. This is a very casual and easy way to make introductions.

It will usually be followed by someone reciprocating by sharing their name and saying hello. It may sound too simple, but it really does work.

Try This:
Start saying hello to all kinds of people – even people you're just passing. Make a little eye contact and say "Hi". Most people find this to be a friendly thing to do and will respond in kind. If they don't, don't take it personally.

TECHNIQUE #5: GIVE SINCERE COMPLIMENTS

Compliments are always a nice way to start a conversation, but it's important that you're sincere when you compliment someone. For example, if you're approaching a speaker from a conference you can say, "I really enjoyed your talk this morning. It really opened up my mind to some new ideas."

Of-course, don't say this if you really disliked the talk! It's always obvious to someone else when you're being insincere. You can try and fake it, but your body language, tone of voice, and facial expressions will give it away. Even if you're a good "faker," people will get a gut feeling that you're being insincere.

So what do you do if you don't have anything specific to compliment? In the case of the speaker whose talk you didn't really love, you could say, "Thank you so much for your talk this morning – I really appreciate the time you took out of your busy schedule."

Here's another example I share in my book, *Persuasion Psychology* (www .AkashKaria.com/Persuasion):

> We tend to like people who like us. I learned this concept first-hand as a high school teenager. When I found out that a girl in my class liked me, I began to like her too - even though previously I hadn't paid much attention to her.
>
> One of the best ways to get someone interested in you is to be interested in them. Similarly, to get someone to like you, you have to like them first.
>
> However, that raises the question: How do you get the other person to realize that you like them?
>
> One of the easiest ways to show people you like them is to compliment them. One study (Drachman, de Carufel and Insko, 1978), found that men who received compliments developed positive feelings towards the person who gave the compliment. This was true even when the men receiving the compliments knew that that the person complimenting them wanted a favor from them.

Next time you want to persuade someone, start by genuinely complimenting them.

If there's absolutely nothing you can compliment with sincerity, it's best to choose a different technique.

Try This:
When you go through your daily interactions, look for ways to compliment people. This is a good practice with the people you already know as well as new people you approach.

TECHNIQUE #6: SOLICIT AN OPINION
How great is it when someone wants to know what *you* think of a particular topic? I love it when someone seems to want my take on a subject.

You can break the ice by asking someone you want to talk to their opinion on a particular subject. For example, one of the questions I use to break the ice at parties is "So, what do you think of the party?" This gets the other person talking, and pretty soon the conversation takes a turns into different, tangential topics (e.g., "Yeah, actually, if you liked the lobster ravioli *here*, you should try out this great place called Seafood and Friends on Central Park! Have you been there before?").

If you're at a business-networking event, you could seek an opinion about any hot topic in your particular industry. It's great to ask about trends and major shifts in the industry.

You can say something like, "What do you think about the changes with ABC association?"

Or if you have a particular project or product on which you're working, you can ask, "Would you mind taking a look at this and letting me know what you think?"

Most people are flattered to have someone else ask about their opinion. In some cases you'll come across someone who truly doesn't have time to peruse your product, but that's not something to take personally. They'll remember that you asked.

Try This:
Consciously ask others for their opinions more often. When you have a new product developed, make sure and get input. This is a good habit and if you really take the opinions seriously you'll also be able to improve what you do.

TECHNIQUE #7: SHARE YOUR PRODUCT

Do you love getting a free product? I know that I always appreciate getting a quality item given to me.

For example, let's say you're attending a conference for writers. If you've written a book, take a few copies with you to give away. It's even better if you sign and personalize them. You may have to spend a little money to give away a product, but it's a small investment that will come back to you in many returns.

Caveat: Be your own judge about when it is and when it isn't appropriate to give away products. In some cases, giving away free products can be a great way of starting up a conversation at networking events (depending on what industry you work in), but in other cases it can come off as too promotional – so be careful when deciding whether or not to use this technique.

Try This:
Develop a product you can share when you meet new people at business events. If you don't have a book, create a short booklet or CD to pass out.

AUTHENTICITY IS CRITICAL

No matter what approach you use, one of the most important things you can do is remain authentic. If you're not sincere it will come across to those around you – and no one really likes someone who comes off like a phony.

The advice to "just be yourself" is as old as time, but it's 100 percent true. You definitely want to avoid pretending that you're someone you are not. Avoid any temptation to stretch the truth about who you are and what you do.

Eventually the truth will come out and you'll be left feeling embarrassed if you've embellished about who you really are. Just be who you are and be the *best* version of you.

ELIMINATING THE FEAR OF APPROACHING SOMEONE NEW

If you're not comfortable with meeting new people, you can build tremendous fear around it. In fact your fear can become so strong that it prevents you from being able to approach someone new.

It's important that you really think about what it is you really fear. Is it:

- Embarrassing yourself by saying something stupid?
- Being rejected?
- A lack of confidence in your abilities and expertise?
- That you don't know what to say or how to behave?

Once you've pinpointed what's actually causing the stress, you can begin to unravel your fears and find it easier to approach someone.

For example, if you're worried that you don't know what to say, you can spend extra time preparing things to say that are relevant and interesting. If you're worried about being rejected, the best way to get over it is to experience rejection and realize that it isn't that bad.

> This advice reminds me of a great sketch from the popular TV sitcom *Friends*. In the episode, Chandler has a fear of commitment – he cannot seem to commit to a relationship. Therefore, his friend Joey offers him these wise words of advice:

"Face your fear. You have a fear of heights? You go to the top of the building. You're afraid of bugs? Get a bug, right? In this case, you have a fear of commitment. So I say you go in there and be the most committed guy there ever was. Oh, yeah. Go for it, man! Jump off the high dive. Stare down the barrel of a gun, pee into the wind!"

So, go ahead and in the wise words of Joey Tribbiani, "pee into the wind!" Face your fears, get rejected, and realize that it's not that bad!

The best way to overcome your fear of approaching someone new is to simply practice. The more you do it the easier it will become – just like most skills and challenges in life.

Begin approaching all kinds of people in a wide variety of situations. If going up to someone you don't know at a business function is too overwhelming, try smaller interactions that don't have so much at stake such as:

- Approaching a stranger and asking for directions.
- Asking for help in a store.
- Making eye contact and saying hello to strangers you pass.

Making a conscious effort to reach out to people you don't know in small ways on a regular basis will make it easier for you to approach new people in any environment – including a business setting.

Over time, your anxiety will naturally fade away. You'll certainly encounter people who aren't interested in you or your message, but each time you experience that type of rejection you'll be able to develop a little thicker skin.

IN A NUTSHELL

- Use your surroundings to break the ice because that's one thing you already have in common.
- Capitalize on current events. Being aware of what's happening in the world will give you extra conversational material to work with.
- Engage your partner in the conversation with open-ended questions.
- Saying "hello" and introducing yourself is usually more than enough to thaw the ice and start a conversation.
- Compliments create liking. If you genuinely like something about someone, then let him/ her know because they'll appreciate you for it.
- People love sharing their thoughts and feelings – so keep your conversational partner engaged by soliciting their opinions on a subject of mutual interest to you both.
- Be yourself – but be the best version of you that you can possibly be!

Chapter 3

HOW TO SEAL A MEMORABLE VERBAL IMPRESSION IN 30 SECONDS

Your non-verbal cues can definitely make an instant first impression, but what you say also has the power to do so. So how do you make sure that you give a great first impression in the first 30 seconds of meeting someone new?

You can look great, but if you don't have something interesting to say when you open your mouth, you can ruin a good first impression.

As an introvert it can be difficult to know exactly what to say, but I've found that by being prepared ahead of time I don't have to have that moment of stammering before I know what words should follow.

TECHNIQUE #1: THE 30-SECOND COMMERCIAL

One of the most important things you can do is develop a quick 30-second commercial that you can share with someone new. This isn't meant to be a long lecture about you – it's just a brief introduction.

Sometimes these 30-second commercials are also called elevator speeches or elevator pitches. What exactly should you plan to say during this time? You need to consider two key points:

- Who you are?
- What makes you unique?

It's important to hit the highlights of who you are and how you can add value to the person with whom you're speaking.

For example, here are my notes for my 30-second commercial:

- Who you are?
  Akash Karia. I'm an author and a professional speaker. I write short books on success and motivation, and travel the world speaking to audiences on how to achieve peak performance.

- What makes you unique?
  I'm of Indian origin, born in Tanzania, studied in Kenya and Hong Kong, and my favorite author is Japanese!

Additionally, for a business-networking event, you should end your 30-second commercial with an open-ended question that helps you to get more information or create a referral. For example, you might ask if they have any suggestions of additional people you might talk to. You might also ask if they have any recommendations or advice for you.

Try This:
Create a basic 30-second commercial for yourself to use during business functions. Here's a great outline to follow as you do this:

- Start with sharing your name and your title or position.
- Create a sentence about your unique strengths and accomplishments.
- Create a sentence about how you can add value to an organization or individual.
- Ask for advice or a referral contact.

TECHNIQUE #2: CREATE CUSTOM COMMERCIALS

It's good to have a basic 30-second commercial that you can use with anyone, anywhere. But if you know that you're going to a specific setting or settings, customize your commercial to fit that setting.

This will help you to keep your introduction fresh and allow you to present information that's relevant to that setting. It's not always possible to prepare ahead of time, but when you can you'll find that it's very beneficial.

For example, you might have a 30-second commercial that's appropriate for a convention and another commercial that you use when you stop by a specific business to market your services.

Before you head out to a specific place, tailor your commercial for that location.

TECHNIQUE #3: MAKE YOUR COMMERCIAL MEMORABLE

Your 30-second commercial won't be effective if no one remembers it. But how do you make sure that what you say isn't forgotten? One way to do this is to use your words to paint a visual picture.

Have you ever been to a presentation that had wonderful visuals? Those pictures can help you to remember the speaker and what he or she discussed. But when you run into someone in a casual setting, you can't show them a PowerPoint presentation.

Instead, you'll need to use what you say to create a mental picture. Then later that person will be able to recall you – he or she may not remember exactly what you said specifically but will remember you.

How can you do this? It helps to actually ask your conversation partners to visualize something. You can ask them to visualize life without the problem that you can solve.

For example, one of the things I do best is help others improve their public speaking skills. So I might say something like, "Imagine standing up in front of a crowd feeling at ease, polished, and confident."

Do you have a picture in your mind? You can imagine yourself on a stage and how it would look and feel. This creates a visual memory.

Later, when someone realizes they have a speech to give and they need some help, they'll remember me as someone who can help them because of the visual memory that was created. They may not remember everything I said, but they got the message that I can help meet their needs.

TECHNIQUE #4: PRACTICE MAKES PERFECT

Once you've developed an engaging 30-second commercial, you'll need to practice it. You don't want to sound too rehearsed, but you also want to be able to quickly recall what you need to say.

Practice your commercial on your own and in the mirror, try it with friends, and then begin putting it into practice. You may stammer a little the first time you give your commercial when it really counts.

But the more you do it, the easier it will get and eventually you'll feel confident and at ease. You'll feel the words flow from you naturally.

TECHNIQUE #5: DON'T RELY TOO HEAVILY ON YOUR COMMERCIAL

It's great to have a 30-second commercial. But what happens if you give your commercial and don't have anything else to say that engages another individual in conversation?

While your commercial is an important way to introduce yourself, it's really only the tip of the iceberg when it comes to who you are and what you do. Don't rely so much on your commercial that you truly have nothing else to say in a conversation.

It's important that you know yourself and the value of your services well enough that you can answer questions and continue a conversation. The commercial is just a jumping-off point to help you get the opportunity to say even more.

TECHNIQUE #6: LISTEN MORE THAN YOU SPEAK

One of the most important elements of your commercial is asking an open-ended question. Remember that when you ask the question you need to stop to listen to the answer.

You might feel anxious and be tempted to start thinking of what you need to say next. But it's much better to really focus on what your conversation partner is saying instead. It's okay to have pauses in conversation.

In the next chapter we'll talk much more about active listening – it's really one of the most important things when it comes to communication.

No one wants to feel like they're not being heard when they speak. By becoming an active listener, you'll help people to feel that you value them and that what they have to say is important to you. This can be one of the best ways to develop a good business and networking relationship – not to mention friendship.

IN A NUTSHELL

- Develop a quick thirty-second commercial that you can share with people at networking events. Answer the questions, "Who are you?" and "What makes you unique?"
- Customize your commercial to fit the setting.
- Don't rely so much on your commercial that you have nothing else to say in a conversation.

Chapter 4

HOW TO BECOME AN ACTIVE LISTENER

Have you ever had a conversation with someone but you could tell they weren't listening to you? Maybe they kept looking down at their phone or you realized that they didn't ask any questions about anything you said.

How did that make you feel? For most people it can be very disheartening to have a one-way conversation. You feel like you don't matter and it's unlikely that you'll ever want to speak to that person again.

Being a great conversationalist often means doing more listening than talking. You want your conversation partner to know that you're paying attention and that what he or she says really matters to you.

CONVERSING VS. CONNECTING

When you're embarking on a conversation with someone new, think about your conversation as more than just words being exchanged. You want to look for connection with the other person.

We've talked a lot about your 30-second introduction and ways to break the ice. But if you get so stuck to those ideas you may miss out on the connection aspect of speaking with someone else.

It's important to be engaged with the other person and not too focused on a "script." Conversation starters are just a jumping-off point – but the meat of your conversation should be active listening.

But what does it really mean to listen actively? Let's explore that further so that you can really apply it to meeting new people and developing key relationships. Getting into this habit will do more for building relationships than just about any other skill.

TECHNIQUE #1: NON-VERBAL CUES

Most of the impact in any conversation comes from nonverbal cues rather than just what is said. You can do several important things to make sure you're providing nonverbal cues that show you're really listening.

Eye Contact

One of the best things you can do is make eye contact.
When you're looking directly at the person in front of you it
shows that you're focused on the conversation. But do not
stare down your conversation partner and make him or her
feel uncomfortable.

In fact, how much eye contact you make is something that
can change depending on the person with whom you're
speaking. For example, someone who is really introverted
might feel uncomfortable with too much eye contact.

But someone who is extroverted and enjoys engaging
conversation may give you the license to make almost
constant eye contact. You'll need to pick up on the other
person's cues to decide what is best.

Head Nodding

When you nod your head in agreement it shows that you are
listening and really hearing what is being said. If you nod
your head almost constantly, though, it can have the
opposite effect.

Save your head nodding for a time when you really
understand and agree with your conversation partner. Don't
become a bobble head who nods without a pause. Have you
ever spoken with someone who nods all the time? Did it
look like they weren't really listening? That's the opposite of
what you want to accomplish.

Smiling

How does it make you feel when someone smiles at you? For most people this can help a conversation to be more relaxed and comfortable. You don't have to smile all the time, but peppering your conversation with plenty of smiles can go a long way to helping another person feel more open in a discussion.

Try This:

When you're working to improve your nonverbal listening skills, it helps to think of someone with whom you really enjoy talking. The next time you talk to them pay attention to the nonverbal cues that they use in conversation.

Do they make frequent eye contact? Do they smile and nod when you're making an excellent point? In your own conversations you can mimic these skills and make them your own over time.

TECHNIQUE #2: REFLECTION AND RESTATEMENT

When someone really hears what you've said, they're able to rephrase it and reflect it back to you. This doesn't mean that they repeat what you've said verbatim, but that they can tell you the essence of what you've said.

Doing this in conversations shows that you're really listening. This technique is particularly helpful when talking to someone who is unhappy with you or just unhappy in general. Many people are upset when they feel they aren't heard.

By using this technique you can show that you hear and understand what the other person is saying to you. That alone can help diffuse difficult situations. What most people really want is to be heard and understood. In other words, they want to feel they matter.

This is a technique that is simple, but it requires practice in order to feel comfortable. The more you do it, the easier it will become.

Try This:
Ask a friend, colleague, or family member to help you practice your active listening skills. Have them tell you a story and then rephrase it and reflect it back to them.

Practice this type of conversation over and over again until it feels natural for you. Ask your conversation partner to critique how well you do or where you can use improvement.

TECHNIQUE #3: ASK QUESTIONS
When you're really interested in a subject and you're talking to an expert, what do you do to get more information? Do you just listen and stop the conversation when the expert is finished speaking? Or do you ask questions and delve deeper into the meat of the subject?

AKASH KARIA

Asking questions is a great way to show your interest in any conversation partner. It shows that you are not only listening intently, but that you want to keep the conversation going and get more information.

This not only helps someone to feel more valued, but it can also really help you to know a person better. It also helps to be genuinely interested in what others have to say – so ask questions only if you're prepared to really listen to the answers.

You don't have to be an expert on any subject in order to ask questions that will provide more details. Here are a few that work well:

- Could you please tell me more about that?
- What did you do next?
- What do you think the outcome will be?
- How did that make you feel?
- What are the next steps?
- What do you wish had gone differently?
- What is your opinion of the situation?

In their book, *What to Talk About: On a Plane, at a Cocktail Party, in a Tiny Elevator with Your Boss's Boss,* authors Chris Colin and Rob Baedeker say that you should "aim for questions that invite people to tell stories, rather than give bland, one-word answers."

Here are some examples that Chris and Rob offer in their blog-post titled *How to Turn Small Talk into Smart Conversation* on TED (www.bit.ly/TED-Conversations):

Instead of . . .
"How are you?"
"How was your day?"
"Where are you from?"
"What do you do?"
"What line of work are you in?"
"What's your name?"
"How was your weekend?"
"What's up?"
"Would you like some wine?"
"How long have you been living here?"

Try . . .
"What's your story?"
"What did you do today?"
"What's the strangest thing about where you grew up?"
"What's the most interesting thing that happened at work today?"
"How'd you end up in your line of work?"
"What does your name mean? What would you like it to mean?"
"What was the best part of your weekend?"
"What are you looking forward to this week?"
"Who do you think is the luckiest person in this room?"

"What does this house remind you of?"
"If you could teleport by blinking your eyes, where would you go right now?"

These questions can be applied to many different situations and conversations. Have a few of them in the back of your mind to pull out when you need to keep the conversation going.

Try This:
Practice asking questions with a conversation partner. Use some of the questions above and develop some of your own. It's important that the questions you ask feel natural and fit into your typical way of speaking.

The next time you find yourself in a conversation, try to add at least one question into the conversation and take note of the results.

TECHNIQUE #4: AVOID DISTRACTIONS
We've all experienced it – for example, you're speaking with someone about something that is important to you and notice that he is looking at his watch, messing with papers on his desk, or even checking emails and text messages. You become deflated realizing that he's not listening and doesn't care at all about what you're saying.

It feels pretty frustrating to be speaking to someone who is completely distracted. Even when someone is interested in you, distractions can make you feel insignificant. As you work to improve your conversation skills it's important to work on minimizing distractions.

Make it a point to avoid activities such as looking at your phone, checking your watch, and fiddling with papers when you're engaged in conversation. If you set up a meeting with another person, do everything you can to put distractions away and focus on the conversation. This, by the way, is a lesson that would have served former US President George Bush well:

> "It wasn't what he said, but rather what his body language said. In the midst of a 1992 presidential debate with Bill Clinton and Ross Perot, [Bush] checked his watch as an audience member was asking a question about the recession.
>
> After checking his watch and straightening his suit jacket, Mr. Bush said: "Of course, you feel it when you're president of the United States; that's why I'm trying to do something about it - by stimulating the export, vesting more, better education system."
>
> The moment showed him to be out of touch with ordinary Americans. While he appeared impatient with the voter, Bill Clinton showed empathy - and won the presidential race." – via The Telegraph (www.bit.ly/Bush-Distraction)

If you're in an impromptu conversation and have important calls and messages coming in (to which you can't wait till later to respond) you can always say, "I'm so sorry. I'm not able to really focus on what you're saying right now. But I really do want to hear more. Can we meet up again in a few minutes?"

This allows you to take care of business while showing the other person that you're really interested in what he or she has to say. It's better to postpone a few minutes to improve the quality of your conversation.

Try This:
Begin paying more attention to the things you're doing during a conversation. If you notice that you're tempted to pick up your phone, place it in a drawer or pocket so that it's not in your hand or right in front of you during a conversation.

If you have a tendency to keep an eye on your computer screen for emails, close your laptop or turn off your monitor during important conversations. Look at the specific distractions that you face and work toward a plan on those specific issues.

TECHNIQUE #5: DON'T INTERRUPT
When you're trying to get a point across and get constant interruptions it can be very frustrating. Likewise you need to

remember to be a courteous listener and minimize your own interruptions.

You may not realize how often you interrupt others because it can become such a habit – and it's very common. Instead of interrupting, focus on keeping your mouth closed and your ears open.

When there's a natural pause in a conversation, you can add your two cents. But until then work on speaking less than you listen.

Try This:
Spend a day focusing on your own listening habits. How often do you find yourself interrupting? Being aware of your weaknesses is the first step towards eliminating them.

TECHNIQUE #6: EMBRACE A PAUSE
It's a pretty natural tendency to try to prepare a response while another person is talking. And while that allows you to quickly get your point across, those thoughts take away from your ability to listen.

A better approach is to listen without worrying about what you will say. Then when you're expected to speak and respond, take a moment to pause. This is the time for you to consider what you'll say next.

We live in a fast-paced world and it may feel a little strange to stop and take a moment to collect your thoughts. But it shows that you're a careful listener and that you are intentional about the way you speak.

Try This:
The more you practice pausing, the less uncomfortable it will become. Take a day or two and focus on just this skill. When someone is talking and you find yourself thinking of what to say next, immediately refocus on the conversation.

TECHNIQUE #7: REFOCUS

It's natural for people to find themselves drifting off during a conversation. You might start thinking about what you need to get done later in the day or even putting together your shopping list in your mind.

When that happens, it's important to refocus. If you're having a particularly boring conversation, a good way to focus is to repeat what the other person is saying silently to yourself.

This technique can help rescue you from a very drab conversation that you need to get through or from a day when you're just tired and your brain is having a hard time focusing on the matter at hand.

Try This:

Watch a documentary movie about a subject that isn't typically exciting for you. Practice repeating what you hear in your mind so that you can stay focused. This will make it easier for you to do the same in conversation.

ACTIVE LISTENING CHANGES RELATIONSHIPS

As you work to improve your active listening skills, you'll begin to see that you develop deeper relationships with all of the people in your life. This helps to strengthen professional networks as well as friendships and family life.

The more you do it, the easier it will become to actively listen in conversations and show that you're interested in the people around you.

IN A NUTSHELL

- Being a great conversationalist is as much about listening as it is about speaking.
- If you truly want to connect with the other person, then you need to become an active listener.
- How you react when the other person is speaking is very important. Use the right non-verbal cues such as eye contact, head nodding and smiling (when appropriate) to encourage the other person to continue talking.
- Use the restatement and reflection technique to make the other person feel heard.
- Ask open-ended questions. It shows that you're listening intently and invites the conversation to keep going.
- Active listening means shutting out distractions. Avoid looking at your phone, checking your watch, and fiddling with papers when you're engaged in conversation.

Chapter 5

HOW TO MAKE YOUR PERSONALITY SHINE

No matter what your personality, you can become someone with a shining personality that attracts others to it. You may not think of yourself as very charismatic. But don't let those feelings of inadequacy get in the way of making your personality shine.

Every person has qualities that are wonderful and we all have a few personality traits that we wish we didn't. But anyone can learn to focus on those positive qualities and even adopt some new ones. You can also learn how to make the good qualities the ones that stand out the most.

BECOMING MORE CHARISMATIC
You've probably heard the term "charismatic" but you might not really understand what it means. Basically, charisma is

made up of the personality traits you have that actually draw people to you.

You may think that charismatic people are just born that way. And it's true that some people naturally have traits and behaviors that make them more engaging. But it's also true that you can learn and develop those traits and behaviors.

It helps to start by knowing which traits are the most important for becoming a charismatic person, professional, and leader.

A study conducted at the University of Minnesota provides us with some important insight into what makes a charismatic leader. This study showed that leaders who had positive emotional expressions were considered the most charismatic leaders.

In turn, those leaders who had positive emotional expressions were shown to have more positive followers – as if their mood was actually contagious. The bottom line? The more positive emotional expressions you have, the more you'll attract others and the more others will follow with a positive mood.

So if you do nothing else as you work to make a good impression, keep things positive! Think about the people that you enjoy spending time with in your own life. Would you rather be around someone who complains all the time and always sees the glass half-empty?

Or would you rather be around someone who is positive and helps you to have an optimistic outlook?

Even if you think you're not very naturally charismatic, making the choice to be more positive will naturally increase your charismatic quotient.

PERSONALITY DO'S AND DON'TS

When you're working on showing off the best aspects of your personality, it helps to follow a few simple rules. Read on for some of the do's and don'ts for making your personality shine.

Do Share Opinions

In order to have a dynamic personality, you'll have to be someone who isn't afraid to share your opinions. That doesn't mean that you have to be aggressive about them.

But don't be afraid to respectfully disagree with someone or share strong views. Just remember that others have the right to their own views. When you become someone who can agree to disagree you'll be more interesting and engaging.

Don't Be Obnoxious and Too Loud

We all know someone who is always too loud and often behaves obnoxiously. Monitor your own volume level and the appropriateness of your behavior.

Many people who are loud and obnoxious are simply unaware of their behavior. You may want to ask some trusted friends or family members if they've noticed you behaving in this way.

It's also particularly important to watch your behavior when you've had alcohol as sometimes people become more obnoxious when they've had too much to drink. (I know a couple of people who could definitely use this advice!)

Do Share Your Passions
People who have passions and talk about them bring a natural spark to a conversation. Make sure that you know your own passions and add them to any discussions you may have.

Don't Be Boring
What does it mean to be boring? Usually someone who is boring tends to talk more than they listen. And they tend to talk about the same things over and over again even when their conversation partners are not engaged.

On the other hand someone who is boring might say nothing at all. The bottom line is that someone who is boring is not engaging in conversation. They might have no opinion on any subject. Your goal is to fall in the middle and be someone who listens, is engaged, and also has opinions.

Do Be Empathetic

Empathy is the ability to understand someone else's feeling as if you've walked a mile in their shoes. It also means being able to lift someone up and support them.

Showing empathy is a wonderful way to engage others. People love to feel that you really understand them and support them. It also helps to understand your own feelings and just be comfortable with talking about feelings in general.

Don't Be Negative

One of the best ways to push people away is to have a negative view of every situation. Remember that charismatic people are positive and uplifting. Strive to be someone who finds the positive in every situation and supports others in positive ways.

That doesn't mean you can't see problems or have a bad day. But it does mean that when you come across a problem you focus on solutions rather than wallowing in self-pity or misery.

Try This:

Spend some time examining your own personality traits. Ask a good friend to describe your personality – both the good and the bad. Then choose one of the negative aspects of your personality and focus on turning it around for the next week.

Over time you'll be able to change bad habits into good ones and embrace a more positive personality that attracts others and helps you to become a charismatic person.

IN A NUTSHELL

- Being charismatic is a skill and just like any skill it can be learned.
- Positivity is one of the main components of charisma.
- Share your opinions, thoughts, feelings and passions, but just remember not to monopolize the conversation.

Chapter 6

GOING FROM INTRODUCTION TO INTIMACY

When you attend a large gathering you may begin with the initial goal of talking to as many people as you can. But in the end, the goal shouldn't be to just meet a lot of people – you also want to begin getting to know people at a deeper level.

You want to create a great first impression, but you also want to create a lasting relationship that can be mutually beneficial. You'll find that when you develop intimacy in your relationships you'll get much more out of them.

TAKING CONVERSATIONS TO THE NEXT LEVEL

It can be a challenge to create conversations that have intimacy in just a few minutes. And while you can't force anyone to like or trust you, you can greatly increase the chances of that happening by following a few simple practices.

TECHNIQUE #1: INVITE APPROACH

Many people put up an invisible wall with their body language that says, "I don't really want to be bothered." In order to invite connection you also need to invite people to approach you.

Smiling and having open body language goes a long way toward doing so. Avoid crossing your arms because it is a signal that says you're not interested in talking. Instead keep your arms loose and near your sides.

If you're uncomfortable with your hands being loose, try holding something such as a book or even a drink. Be aware of your facial expressions and keep them friendly and light.

Try This:
Look at yourself in the mirror with different postures and expressions. Try to assume an approachable position and then pay attention to how your body feels. At a function you won't have a mirror to see your posture and facial expressions so you'll want to know how they physically feel.

TECHNIQUE #2: AVOID JUDGMENT

When someone makes a snap judgment about you it can be untrue and hurt your chances of having a good relationship. The same is true when you make a snap judgment about someone else.

Look at everyone you approach as a discovery to be made. Remember that you don't know much about someone until you've spent some time talking and getting to know them.

You may find that you really don't enjoy every person that you meet, but almost everyone has an interesting point of view and background story. Make an effort to get to know someone rather than judging a book by its cover.

Try This:
When you find yourself making a snap judgment about someone (and most of us do this at least to some degree), think of the beginning of a book. Consider that you just need to keep reading and getting to know this person more before coming to any conclusions.

TECHNIQUE #3: BE GENUINE

Have you ever been approached by a salesperson? Many people who are in sales are very good at approaching new people, but it can be pretty obvious from the beginning that they're not as interested in you as they are in making a sale. Of course, this doesn't apply to all salespeople (I know a lot of great salespeople who genuinely care about their products and their customers), but there are a few too many salespeople who value making a quick buck over building a relationship.

The best salespeople actually come across as genuinely interested in you and put the sale as a secondary motive. As you develop a relationship, you become more interested in purchasing a product from a particular person because of who they are.

In my experience, I have found this to be true. Currently, I work as the Chief Commercial Officer of a multimillion-dollar company in East Africa. Every year, I interview, hire, and fire salespeople – and I've found that the best-performing salespeople are not those who place priorities on making immediate sales, but those who focus on meeting and building relationships with the decision-makers.

In order to be genuine you need to be yourself and you also need to be sincerely interested in the other person. When you're not being sincere it will be obvious to most people.

Being genuine will help people to feel more comfortable with you and be more interested in a relationship with you. Avoid the temptation to tell a story that isn't completely true or try to be anyone that you're not.

Try This:
When you're talking to someone, employ active listening techniques that show you're interested in them. Think about

someone who comes across as very genuine to you and list the traits that make them so sincere. Try to model some of those traits and incorporate them into who you are.

TECHNIQUE #4: ASK FOR HELP

One way to develop connection with someone is to ask them for assistance. Most people enjoy feeling needed and helpful. Look for ways that you can ask others to assist you. Benjamin Franklin, for example, used this technique to win the friendship of a man who had previously been very opposed to him. In his autobiography, Franklin writes:

> "Having heard that he had in his library a certain very scarce and curious book, I wrote a note to him expressing my desire of perusing that book and requesting he would do me the favour of lending it to me for a few days.
>
> He sent it immediately – and I returned it in about a week with another note expressing strongly my sense of the favour. When we next met in the House, he spoke to me (which he had never done before), and with great civility. And he ever afterward manifested a readiness to serve me on all occasions, so that we became great friends, and our friendship continued to his death.
>
> This is another instance of the truth of an old maxim I had learned, which says, 'He that has once done

you a kindness will be more ready to do you another than he whom you yourself have obliged.'"

Ask people for feedback about your business or service and be open to any constructive criticism that you receive. Asking for help or even just for someone's opinion can be very powerful.

Try This:
Come up with a list of specific things you need so that you're ready to ask for assistance. For example, you might ask for help in expanding your network, shaping a particular part of your business, or looking for local resources to support a current need.

TECHNIQUE #5: ASK HOW YOU CAN HELP
Just as it's beneficial to ask for assistance and allow others to feel needed and valuable, you can also ask what you can do for others. Ask open-ended questions such as "What can I do to support you?"

In her blog-post titled *To Make a Friend, Ask Someone For a Favor*, New York Times bestselling author Gretchen Rubin writes:

> "Studies show that for happiness, *providing* support is just as important as *getting* support. By offering people a way to provide support, you generate good feelings in them.

So asking, and receiving, a favor generates good feelings on both sides.

Obviously, there are small favors and big favors. You don't want to ask someone to take care of your dog while you're on vacation unless that person is already a CLOSE friend. But asking for a recommendation for a good dentist isn't burdensome." – via Gretchen Rubin (www.GretchenRubin.com)

You may be surprised by the needs that people express – often they're quite different than what you might have assumed. By supporting people in the ways that are needed you become more valuable.

Spend a day focused on serving and supporting others. If people ask for help that you're not able to provide yourself, help them find someone who can do it. Pay attention to the shift that you see in your relationships as you offer to help with no strings attached.

BE PERSONAL

Often in professional relationships we work very hard to come off as polished and appropriate. Sometimes that focus on professionalism puts up an artificial barrier to relationships.

But it's okay – and even good – to be personal in early conversations. That can mean joking around or talking about something personal to ease some of the tension and create a meaningful connection.

Try This:
When you're having a conversation and you notice that you share a similarity, share a personal story about an experience you've had. Look for ways to personalize conversations and take them from superficial to true connection.

VENTURE INTO ASKING PERSONAL QUESTIONS

In a study conducted by psychologist Arthur Aron, "Aron separated two groups of people, then paired people up within their groups and had them chat with one another for 45 minutes. While the first group of pairs spent the 45 minutes engaging in small talk, the second group got a list of questions that gradually grew more intimate. Not surprisingly, the pairs who asked the gradually more probing questions felt closer and more connected after the 45 minutes were up." – via Business Insider (www.bit.ly/Aron-Study)

The key takeaway here is that if you want to build rapport and develop a sense of connectedness with the other person, you should not be afraid to gradually venture into more personal questions. To help you out, here are the thirty-six questions that Aron used as part of the study (via Business Insider - www.bit.ly/36-Questions):

1. Given the choice of anyone in the world, whom would you want as a dinner guest?

2. Would you like to be famous? In what way?

3. Before making a phone call, do you ever rehearse what you're going to say? Why?

4. What would constitute a perfect day for you?

5. When did you last sing to yourself? To someone else?

6. If you were able to live to the age of 90 and retain either the mind or body of a 30-year old for the last 60 years of your life, which would you choose?

7. Do you have a secret hunch about how you will die?

8. Name three things you and your partner appear to have in common.

9. For what in your life do you feel most grateful?

10. If you could change anything about the way you were raised, what would it be?

11. Take four minutes and tell you partner your life story in as much detail as possible.

12. If you could wake up tomorrow having gained one quality or ability, what would it be?

13. If a crystal ball could tell you the truth about yourself, your life, the future or anything else, what would you want to know?

14. Is there something that you've dreamt of doing for a long time? Why haven't you done it?

15. What is the greatest accomplishment of your life?

16. What do you value most in a friendship?

17. What is your most treasured memory?

18. What is your most terrible memory?

19. If you knew that in one year you would die suddenly, would you change anything about the way you are now living? Why?

20. What does friendship mean to you?

21. What roles do love and affection play in your life?

22. Alternate sharing something you consider a positive characteristic of your partner. Share a total of five items.

23. How close and warm is your family? Do you feel your childhood was happier than most other people's?

24. How do you feel about your relationship with your mother?

25. Make three true "we" statements each. For instance, "we are both in this room feeling..."

26. Complete this sentence "I wish I had someone with whom I could share..."

27. If you were going to become a close friend with your partner, please share what would be important for him or her to know.

28. Tell your partner what you like about them: be honest this time, saying things that you might not say to someone you've just met.

29. Share with your partner an embarrassing moment in your life.

30. When did you last cry in front of another person? By yourself?

31. Tell your partner something that you like about them already.

32. What, if anything, is too serious to be joked about?

33. If you were to die this evening with no opportunity to communicate with anyone, what would you most regret not having told someone? Why haven't you told them yet?

34. Your house, containing everything you own, catches fire. After saving your loved ones and pets, you have time to safely make a final dash to save any one item. What would it be? Why?

35. Of all the people in your family, whose death would you find most disturbing? Why?

36. Share a personal problem and ask your partner's advice on how he or she might handle it. Also, ask your partner to reflect back to you how you seem to be feeling about the problem you have chosen.

Now, just as important as asking personal questions and sharing personal stories is *how* you react to the other person's disclosure. In fact, "There's some wonderful work by Harry Reis and his colleagues on self-disclosure showing it's not how much is disclosed but how you respond to the other person's self-disclosure. You want to be very responsive to hear what they're saying, to show that you understand it, to show that you value what they're saying and appreciate it." – via Bakadesuyo (www.Bakadesuyo.com)

AGREE TO DISAGREE

You're not always going to agree with other people. Avoid the temptation to agree simply to create a connection. As your relationship progresses it will be more difficult to maintain a false opinion.

Instead, be willing to disagree but do so gently. Share your opinions but also accept the opinions of others. Many people enjoy lively discussions with differing views. This creates connection rather than opposition when you handle every topic with respect.

Don't make it personal when someone disagrees with your opinion. Instead, look at it as an opportunity to get a new perspective – even if you don't agree with it.

Practice this principle with your current relationships. Introduce hot-button topics, then work to listen to another's opinion and share yours without becoming personal or negative. The more you do this, the easier it will get for you. Once you feel comfortable agreeing to disagree with your established friends you can begin doing so with new acquaintances.

In fact, research conducted by Dan Ariely revealed that controversial, hot-button topics actually make for more interesting conversations than bland, boring ones:

> "Our daters had to choose questions from the list to ask another dater, and could not ask anything else. They were forced to risk it by posing questions that

are considered outside of generally accepted bounds. And their partners responded, creating much livelier conversations than we had seen when daters came up with their own questions. Instead of talking about the World Cup or their favorite desserts, they shared their innermost fears or told the story of losing their virginity. Everyone, both sender and replier, was happier with the interaction.

And what can you do personally with this idea? Think about what you can do to make sure that your discussions are not the boring but not risky type. Maybe set the rules of discussion upfront and get your partner to agree that tonight you will only ask questions and talk about things you are truly interested in. Maybe you can agree to ask 5 difficult questions first, instead of wasting time talking about your favorite colors. Or maybe we can create a list of topics that are not allowed. By forcing people to step out of their comfort zone, risk tipping the relationship equilibria, we might ultimately gain more." – via Dan Ariely (www.DanAriely.com)

As the research shows, don't be frightened of talking about controversial topics.

TECHNIQUE #3: LET FRIENDSHIP FLOW NATURALLY

Are there any friends in your current circle who were difficult to get to know? Chances are you know someone who was very guarded and took more time to open up to you. It's important that you respect the boundaries that others set.

Avoid being pushy or overbearing. Ultimately you want people to naturally open up to you rather than you having to pry them open with force. By practicing the principles in this chapter you'll find that most people will eventually warm up to you.

Be patient, but also be persistent. It can be tempting to give up on a relationship that doesn't seem to be going anywhere. But with patience even the toughest people can become powerful allies.

IN A NUTSHELL

- Closed body language puts up an invisible wall between you and your conversational partner. Instead, use open body language to invite conversation.
- Be genuinely interested in the other person. The more interested you are in them, the more interested they will be in you.
- Don't be afraid to ask for help, and also ask how *you* can help.
- To deepen the relationship, slowly ease into asking personal questions and sharing more personal information (such as your dreams, hopes, fears, etc.)
- Controversial topics are fine to bring up as long as you are respectful and do not force your opinions on others. In fact, research by Dan Ariely revealed that controversial, hot-button topics make for more interesting conversations than bland, boring ones.

Chapter 7

HOW TO KEEP YOUR CONVERSATION ALIVE

We've all had conversations that seemed to start off great but were followed by the dreaded awkward silence. What you do in that moment can make or break your conversation.

DON'T BE TOO AFRAID OF SILENCE

Sometimes it's okay to have silence in your conversations. The best of friends can actually enjoy time together without having to fill every moment with words. Sometimes a conversation can have silence that isn't awkward at all.

Silence can signal that one person in the conversation is really thinking about a topic before speaking on it. But there are times when silence goes on too long and begins to feel awkward.

Both people in the conversation might be trying to think of what to say next or even how to get away from the person to whom they're talking. If you are feeling strange or awkward, chances are the other person is feeling it too.

SAVING A DYING CONVERSATION

When a dreaded lull comes to your conversation, you can do several things to save it and bring it back to life. Read on for a few easy tips to steer things back to the right direction.

Go Back to the Beginning

Remember the skills it took to strike up a conversation in the first place? Those same skills can help revive a discussion. Choose a new subject or comment on something that will give you something else to talk about.

Tackle Transition Topics

There are many transition topics that can give you something to talk about and breathe fresh air into your discussion. Some examples include:

- **Hobbies:** Look for hobbies that you have in common or that are just interesting to discuss. This could be reading great books, playing sports, doing creative arts, or going on outdoor adventures.

On that note, it helps to be someone who has a few interesting hobbies. If you spend all of your time working, you may come across as a bit dull. Take some time to develop an interest or two outside of your profession if you haven't already done so.

- **Local Flavor:** When you're looking for something to discuss, take advantage of the local scene. You can talk about some local events, sports teams, news, or landmarks. If you're visiting a new area, a local person will love to tell you about local attractions. If you're in your own city, be prepared to share some of the most popular attractions in your area. This can give you something to talk about that's interesting and appropriate for a new friend.

- **Professional Events:** If you're attending a conference you can discuss some of the workshops you've attended. You may also be able to bring up future events such as conferences, meetings, or mixers. You can also talk about current issues in your profession such as your professional organization, trends, and market changes. Bringing up a new topic can give you more to talk about and help you move forward from an awkward silence.

State the Obvious

Sometimes you can get through an awkward silence by pointing it out in a humorous way. Calling out what's happening can help both of you feel more relaxed and help you to move forward.

Change the Focus
Another way you can get a conversation going again is to turn it back toward your speaking partner. Most people love to talk about themselves and this can keep things going.

However, you do want to avoid asking questions in a way that feels like an interrogation. Keep things light and use open-ended questions as a way to free up the conversation without making the other person feel uncomfortable.

IS THE CONVERSATION OVER?
Sometimes a lull in the conversation is just a natural signal that the conversation has reached a conclusion. Sure, you could keep it going if you wanted to but there really isn't a need to do so.

When that happens, you'll want to use the lull as a tool for ending the conversation in a positive way. In Chapter 9 I'll share my best tips for doing this.

IN A NUTSHELL

- Silence doesn't have to be uncomfortable. Sometimes, silence is welcome in a conversation. Not every pause has to be filled with words.
- To keep a conversation alive, transition into new topics that may be of genuine interest to you both.
- Use open-ended questions and put the focus on your partner, inviting them to share more of themselves with you.

Chapter 8

HOW TO AVOID STOPPING A CONVERSATION COLD

You've probably heard that you should avoid talking about politics or religion in social settings – especially with new people. And while these can be hot-button issues, they're certainly not the only topics that can cause a conversation to come to a screeching halt.

AVOID THESE TOPICS IN CONVERSATION

Quite a few topics are considered in appropriate in many situations. Make sure you avoid them if you want to leave your company with a good impression.

> Side note: The following topics may be fine once you get to know someone and have developed a good relationship with them. However, generally speaking, you want to avoid them when you're meeting someone for the first time.

SEX

Sex is not a topic that should be discussed in casual conversation – especially with people you don't know well, and especially in professional settings. Discussing sexual conquests or making sexual jokes will be a major turn-off.

OFFENSIVE HUMOR

Offensive humor includes sexual jokes, but is not limited to them. You'll also want to avoid making jokes about bodily functions, ethnicity, or gender stereotypes. These are all offensive in their own ways.

Avoid any type of controversial humor until you know someone well and know their taste in jokes.

FINANCES

When you're talking with close friends the topic of finances is usually acceptable. But when you're talking to someone new, discussing money can be awkward. This includes talking about your salary, telling how much you paid for things, and asking other people questions about their financial situations.

You should also avoid talking about others' finances and spreading gossip. Note that when someone does share financial information with you, it's not your information to share with others.

HEALTH ISSUES

Some health topics are perfect for casual conversation. You might feel comfortable discussing organic foods or your favorite form of exercise. But when it comes to more specific matters it's best to keep health information out of a friendly conversation with acquaintances.

For example, it's best not to discuss chronic illness, surgeries, or major injuries. Bringing this up can make people feel uncomfortable and can take a light-hearted atmosphere and make it too serious.

Avoid discussions of body fluids, functions, and other things that might make some people squeamish. This is especially true if you're having a conversation at a meal.

While it might not bother you to talk about these things, many people are uncomfortable and even disgusted by this type of conversation.

These are the most critical topics to avoid. By bringing up these topics you're likely to make people feel uncomfortable and cut off a relationship that could have potentially benefited you.

CONVERSATION KILLERS

We've discussed topics that you should avoid, but it's also important to know behaviors that can bring a conversation to stop. Pay careful attention to your actions to avoid awkward endings.

MONOPOLIZING

You've probably been at a party and noticed that one person tends to monopolize the conversation. For example, one woman always has something to say about every topic and always has a personal experience that she must share.

You've probably also noticed that people tend to try to get away from this type of person and you may even find yourself rolling your eyes and looking for escape routes. No one likes it when someone spends too much time talking about themselves and takes over the conversation.

FORCING YOUR OPINIONS ON OTHERS

We've talked a lot about learning to agree to disagree. The opposite of that is having strong opinions and trying to force them on others. You can also lose friendships by being very judgmental about others' opinions and personally attacking them.

For example, you can disagree on a topic but it's inappropriate to say that a person is an idiot ("You're an idiot for thinking that!" or "You don't know what you're talking about!") because his or her opinion differs from yours. People who judge in this way have a difficult time maintaining positive working relationships and friendships.

DISTRACTED BODY LANGUAGE

When you're not listening to your conversation partner, he or she has no reason to continue talking. Checking your watch, appearing bored, and allowing other distractions to grab your attention is a great way to end a conversation.

Instead, always focus on maintaining active listening techniques to avoid this problem when you're working to develop new relationships.

NEGATIVITY

We've discussed this earlier, but it bears repeating. You will have a hard time being seen as a leader and someone who can be trusted if you're constantly negative. People may be willing to be around you for a little while, but the negativity will eventually get old and push people away.

Being negative all the time can be a habit – and one that's tough to break. But it is possible to break the habit and become a more positive, optimistic person. If you struggle with negativity (as I did), then you can check out my book *Anti-Negativity: How to Stop Negative Thinking and Start Living a Positive Life* on www.AkashKaria.com/AntiNegativity

PROFANITY

This is in the same vein as using offensive humor. For some people profanity isn't offensive but for others it is. It's rarely appropriate to use profanity in conversations in a professional setting.

If you tend to use a lot of profanity, you may not notice how much you do it. Become hyper aware of your language and work to clean it up. Less is more when it comes to strong language.

Some behaviors that are acceptable in your home or at the local pub with friends are not acceptable at work. Profanity is one of those behaviors that you need to keep in check.

FISHING FOR COMPLIMENTS

While you don't want to come across as arrogant in conversations, you also want to avoid taking it too far the other way and constantly putting yourself down. This type of talk makes it seem that you're fishing for compliments.

It's okay to be a little self-deprecating – in fact that can be a sign of humility. But if you're always saying negative things about yourself it can become tiresome and will push people away.

WHAT TO DO WHEN YOU MAKE A MISTAKE

It can take a long time to correct a bad impression, but it's possible to do so. The best thing you can do is work hard to correct negative behaviors that cause problems in the first place.

But if you happen to insert your foot into your mouth, you can recover.

First, admit your mistake to the person you've offended. Being honest and willing to admit imperfections shows humility.

Next, apologize for any offense that was caused. Saying "I'm sorry" can go a long way toward mending fences. If you've made a major faux pas, ask what you can do to repair the situation.

For example, if you offended a larger group of people or caused a problem at an event, you may need to send notes of apology or apologize to the leader of the group. You could also help organize a future event and use service as a way to make amends.

Finally, reach out in appropriate ways in the future. And make sure that you learn from your mistake and correct the inappropriate behavior.

IN A NUTSHELL

- Sex, offensive humor and profanity can quickly dampen a good conversation.
- Health and financial problems are two topics you should avoid.
- Monopolizing the conversation, fishing for compliments and forcing your opinion on others will bury a conversation alive.
- Negativity is a big no-no. No matter how much you want to vent and complain, remember that no one likes being around a negative person.
- When you make a mistake, take full responsibility and apologize for any offense caused.

Chapter 9

HOW TO END THE CONVERSATION POSITIVELY

The purpose of striking up new conversations is to create new connections beyond just that moment. How you end a conversation is as important as how you begin it. You want to leave your new acquaintance with a favorable impression of you going forward.

WHEN SHOULD YOU END A CONVERSATION?

Ending a conversation can be an art form. You don't want to end it abruptly in a way that causes someone to feel unimportant. Instead, learn to gracefully end a conversation. Here are three opportunities to do that:

Natural Pause

In a conversation when the passion for the current topic has died down, there's often a natural pause. This is usually a great time to end a conversation and move on to a new person or activity.

Awkward Pause

If you're in the situation of having an awkward pause in conversation, it may be best to politely end the conversation – especially if efforts to revive the discussion have failed.

Event Transition

If you're attending a professional meeting or conference, there will be built-in times for transition. For example, you may end a conversation as a speaker is getting ready to begin or the next session is about to start.

ENDING ON THE RIGHT NOTE

When it's time to end a conversation, there are a few steps that can help you to do so gracefully and leave a great last impression. This will make it easier for you to follow up later.

STEP 1: GIVE YOUR REASON FOR NEEDING TO LEAVE

When it's time to end the conversation, provide a reason for needing to leave. For example you might say "It's almost time for the keynote address" or "I have an appointment that I need to get to."

Giving a reason gives the impression that you'd love to keep talking, but you really can't.

STEP 2: EXPRESS APPRECIATION

After giving your reason, make sure that you express appreciation for the discussion. Saying "It was so nice to meet you" or "I'm so glad I bumped into you today!" will show that you enjoyed the new connection.

STEP 3: POSITIVE REFLECTION

You'll also want to make a positive comment about something that you've discussed. This is another way to confirm that you've been actively listening to the conversation. For example, you might say something like "Good luck with your meeting next week! I can't wait to hear how it goes."

STEP 4: EXCHANGE INFORMATION (OPTIONAL)

Sometimes you meet someone that you enjoy talking to, but don't really plan to see again. But often you'll want to see a new person again so it's important to make that possible.

Make sure that you exchange contacts. For professional events, always keep business cards with you so that you can have a way to quickly exchange information.

STEP 5: SUGGEST A FUTURE MEETING (OPTIONAL)

If you want to see someone again, go ahead and suggest getting together in the future. You might say, "I'd love to meet up again and continue this discussion next week. How does lunch on Friday sound?" This keeps the door open for future connections.

A GOOD LAST IMPRESSION

We spend a lot of time talking about making a good first impression. But your last impression is almost as important. When you leave someone you want it to be a positive experience that leaves the door open for a developing relationship.

Don't put in great effort to provide a great first impression, and then abruptly end a conversation in a negative way. Instead, leave someone feeling that they mattered, that they're interesting to you, and that you want to know more.

IN A NUTSHELL

- The two best times to end a conversation are:
    - Pauses in the conversation.
    - Event transitions.
- When you have to exit a conversation, give a reason for having to do so.
- Expressing appreciation for the conversation makes the other person feel good for having connected with you.
- Make a positive comment about something you've discussed to show that you enjoyed the conversation.
- Swap contacts and suggest a future meeting if you'd like to continue the relationship in the future.

Chapter 10

FOLLOWING UP ON A CONVERSATION TO DEEPEN THE RELATIONSHIP

Making a great impression with someone new is a critical task when you're networking. But it's not enough to have an initial contact if you want to create a network of people from which you can truly benefit personally and professionally.

Following up is a key practice that can make or break your efforts. After the initial conversation, you can follow up in order to develop a true relationship.

TAKE NOTES
When you're meeting a lot of new people, it can be hard to keep the details straight. It helps to take notes right away so that you don't have to commit details to memory.

When you have a conversation with someone and get their card, take a moment or two to write a few notes on the back to refresh your memory later. If you don't get a card, enter contact information into your phone or write it on a notepad along with a few details.

Later you can go back to these notes and they'll help you as you make future contacts and establish deeper relationships.

TAKE THE FIRST STEP
Don't wait for someone else to contact you if you're interested in creating a stronger connection. You can make a quick follow-up via a phone call or even an email.

DON'T WAIT TOO LONG TO FOLLOW UP
If you wait weeks or months the other person may have forgotten who you are. Make sure you follow up within a week of the first meeting.

Also, don't wait until you need something to make that first contact. You don't want to come across as someone who's only interested in what's in it for you.

GIVE REMINDERS
When you reach out to contact someone you met briefly, make sure to remind them of when and where you met.

They may have met a hundred new people in a week and need something specific to refresh their memory.

FOLLOW UP ON SOMETHING YOU DISCUSSED

When you reach out in the follow-up contact, bring up something related to your initial conversation. For example, if you discussed an upcoming meeting or presentation ask how it went.

SET UP A MEETING

While it isn't always necessary, this is a good time to set up a next meeting with someone you'd like to see again. This could be lunch, coffee, or even a dinner.

Getting to meet with someone in person will help strengthen the relationship and allow you to establish a connection that is more meaningful.

MOVING FORWARD WITH YOUR RELATIONSHIP

It's important to have good initial conversations, but they won't do much for you if you don't follow up. A good conversation is a good starting point, but you'll want to nurture the seed you've planted in order to grow your network.

You can do this by following up quickly and creating future opportunities to work with your new contacts. You also need to make sure that you follow through on any commitments that you make.

For example, if you discuss wanting to help out at the next conference make sure that you're really willing to do what you offered. The more you follow through with your commitments and keep in contact with your new acquaintances, the more likely you are to develop solid business relationships and friendships.

IN A NUTSHELL

- Keep notes about people you meet so that you can refresh your memory if you do decide to have a second meeting.
- Don't wait more than a week to follow-up. The longer you wait to talk to someone, the colder that relationship becomes.
- If you wait until you need something from the other person, then you'll be perceived as being selfish and manipulative.
- Be the first one to reach out – the other person will appreciate you for it.
- Bring up something related to your initial conversation. This is a good way to pick up where you left off.
- Suggest a meeting time and date. The more often you meet someone, the stronger that relationship becomes.

Chapter 11

WRAP UP

Wow, that's a lot of tools for such a little book. And yes, while this is a tiny book, don't let that fool you: the techniques you've just picked up are very powerful and will get you big results!

Because there are so many tools covered in this book, this chapter will serve as a useful checklist on your journey to becoming a more charismatic and confident you. Read the summary below, and then come back several weeks later and re-read it to keep the techniques fresh in your mind:

1 – It only takes a tenth of a second to make an accurate judgment about someone you meet or see. In one study, participants who watched less than a one-second video of political candidates were able to correctly predict 70% of the time who would win the election.

2 – If you want to make a great first impression, make a conscious decision to be enthusiastic! Researchers have

found that focusing on trying to be happy can make you happy. Similarly, making a conscious choice to be enthusiastic will make you more enthusiastic.

3 – If you're feeling anxious, try snapping your fingers to "snap" yourself out of the anxiety. This helps to break up nervous energy and allows you to refocus on becoming enthusiastic instead.

4 – Exercise is another way to help use up nervous energy and promote a more relaxed, but enthusiastic energy. Before a big event try going for a ten-minute walk or jog.

5 – Be aware of your posture. How you hold yourself says a lot about how you feel – even though this may be an unconscious message.

6 – Envision someone who embodies the charisma, confidence and social skills you aspire to. Visualize how that person's posture: how do they stand? What do you notice about their movement? Next, model that same posture. Notice all the adjustments you have to make in order to take on that posture.

7 – Before going to your next event, stand in a high-confidence posture for at least two minutes. Your head should be held high, your shoulders back, and your chest out. The high-confidence posture has been scientifically proven to increase your confidence and decrease your stress levels.

8 – Avoid putting an invisible wall with your body language that says, "I don't want to talk to you". Avoid crossing your arms because it is a signal that says you're not interested in talking. Instead, adopt an open posture to welcome conversation.

9 – Smile because it's contagious. When someone smiles at you, you feel compelled to smile back. Smiling puts everyone in a positive mood, which creates liking.

10 – Eye contact is so powerful that it can even make people fall in love with you. A study conducted in 1989 and published in the Journal of Research in Personality found that there's a major connection between eye contact and passion.

11 – If you struggle with making eye contact when you meet someone new, try turning it into a little game. Challenge yourself to pay attention to the other person's eye color.

12 – Dress to impress. Whether you like it or not, people form judgments about you based on how you dress. Go to the tailor and get your clothes adjusted to fit you just perfectly. A tailor can take in sleeves or waistbands that are too big and give you the perfect fit.

13 – One of the easiest ways to start a new conversation is to use your surroundings. Given that you're both in the same place, you instantly have one thing in common to talk about.

14 – Capitalize on current events. Before you attend any major event where you know you want to network, make sure that you spend some time catching up on current events because this gives you some extra material to work with.

15 – Ask open-ended questions to engage the other person in conversation.

16 – The best way to break the ice is to just say "Hello" and introduce yourself. If you want to practice, start saying hello to all kinds of people – even people you're just passing.

17 – Compliments are always a nice way to start a conversation, but it's important that you're sincere when you give a compliment. If you genuinely like something about someone, let them know.

18 – Break the ice by soliciting people's opinions on a topic of interest. This can be as simple as asking, "So, how do you find the event so far?" or "How do you like the food?"

19 – Develop a quick 30-second commercial that you can share with someone new. Include the answers to the questions, "Who are you?" and "What makes you unique?"

20 – Customize your commercial to fit the setting you will be in. This will keep your introduction fresh and allow you to present information that's relevant to that setting.

21 – Don't over-rely on your commercial. While your commercial is an important way to introduce yourself, it's only the tip of the iceberg when it comes to who you are and what you do. Don't rely so much on your commercial that you truly have nothing else to say in a conversation.

22 – When you're embarking on a conversation with someone new, think about your conversation as more than just words being exchanged. You want to look for a connection with the other person.

23 – Provide the right non-verbal cues to show that you're listening.

24 – Many people are upset when they feel they aren't heard. Use the reflection and restatement technique to show your conversational partner that you understand and care about they're saying.

25 – Ask open-ended questions such as "How did that make you feel?", "What was that like?" and "What happened next?" to gain more information and keep the conversation going.

26 – Avoid distractions. Make it a point to avoid activities such as looking at your phone, checking your watch, and fiddling with papers when you're engaged in conversation.

27 – Avoid the urge to interrupt and butt in with your story/opinion. Instead of interrupting, focus on keeping your mouth closed and your ears open.

28 – Focus on paying attention to what's being said instead of trying to form your own responses when your conversational partner is speaking.

29 – Refocus when you find your attention drifting. It's natural for people to find themselves drifting off during a conversation. When that happens, consciously tune back into the conversation.

30 – A study by the University of Minnesota revealed that leaders who had positive emotional expressions were considered the most charismatic leaders. If you want to be charismatic, focus on being positive.

31 – Share your opinions. We're attracted to those who are not afraid of expressing themselves and their view of the world because it allows us to learn from them.

32 – Share your passions. What are you passionate about? Share that with your listeners. Your passion is contagious and will leave the other person feeling energized.

33 – Make an effort to be genuinely interested in the other person. When we are interested in others, they reciprocate by showing interest in us.

34 – If you want to build intimacy and a close connection with your conversational partner, slowly ease into asking personal questions and sharing more information that is personal in nature (such as your dreams, hopes, fears, etc.)

35 – Don't be frightened to bring up controversial topics. Research by Dan Ariely revealed that controversial, hot-button topics make for more interesting conversations than bland, boring ones.

36 – Understand that sometimes silence is okay. The best of friends can actually enjoy time together without having to fill every moment with words.

37 – To keep a conversation alive, transition into new topics that may be of genuine interest to both of you.

38 – To resuscitate a dying conversation, use an open-ended question and put the focus on your partner, inviting them to share more of themselves with you.

39 – Sex, offensive humor, health and financial issues are topics that can bring a good conversation to a screeching halt.

40 – Avoid monopolizing the conversation. A good conversation is a balanced game of 'back-and-forth'.

41 – Negativity, profanity and distracted body language will immediately kill almost any conversation.

42 – To end a conversation, look for a pause in the conversation or an event transition.

43 – When it's time to end the conversation, provide a reason for needing to leave. Giving a reason gives the impression that you'd love to keep talking, but you really can't.

44 – Express appreciation for conversation to show that you enjoyed the new connection.

45 – Provide positive reflection and make a positive comment about something that you've discussed to let the other person know that you were actually listening.

46 – Exchange information and suggest a future meeting date if you'd like to deepen the relationship over further meetings.

47 – To further the connection, take the first step and reach out via a quick phone-call or email message.

48 - Make sure you follow up within a week of the first meeting. Don't wait until you need something to make that first contact because this will not be perceived positively.

49 – When following up, remind the other person of when and where you met to refresh their memory.

50 – During the follow-up, bring up something related to your initial conversation. This naturally picks up the conversation from where you left off.

51 – Remember that mastering these techniques takes practice. Put into practice the exercises and suggestions in this book, and step-by-step watch yourself grow into a more confident, charismatic and socially-savvy you.

ONE LAST THING

Now that you're done reading the book, here's what I want you to do: I want you to relax, sit back and imagine yourself at a social situation, surrounded by a group of people. Imagine them smiling and enthusiastic. Imagine them being hooked onto your every word. Imagine them fully engaged in what you're saying. Picture yourself being genuinely interested in them and what they have to say.

Imagine yourself enthusiastic, totally confident and enjoying the moment.

To your social success,

Akash Karia
www.AkashKaria.com

QUESTIONS OR COMMENTS?

I'd love to hear your thoughts. Email me on: akash.speaker@gmail.com

INTERESTED IN HAVING ME SPEAK AT YOUR NEXT EVENT?

I deliver high-impact keynotes and workshops on productivity, time management, success psychology and effective communication. Check out the full list of my training programs on www.AkashKaria.com/keynotes and reach me on akash.speaker@gmail.com to discuss how we can work together.

GRAB $297 WORTH OF FREE RESOURCES

Want to learn the small but powerful hacks to make you insanely productive?

Want to discover the scientifically proven techniques to ignite your influence?

Interested in mastering the art of public speaking and charisma?

Then head over to www.AkashKaria.com to grab your free "10X Success Toolkit" (free MP3s, eBooks and videos designed to unleash your excellence). Be sure to sign up for the newsletter and join over 11,800 of your peers to receive free, exclusive content that I don't share on my blog.

YOU MIGHT ALSO ENJOY

If you enjoyed this book, then check out Akash's other books:

HOW SUCCESSFUL PEOPLE THINK DIFFERENTLY

"This book is packed with really wonderful mindsets, reframes, and psychology tips, all backed with references and real science. This is like the "best of the best" self-help tips. A quick read, but a thanksgiving feast of food for thought."
~ Tim Brennan, #1 Bestselling Author of '1001 Chess Tactics'

Grab the book here:
www.AkashKaria.com/SuccessBook

PERSUASION PSYCHOLOGY: 26 POWERFUL TECHNIQUES TO PERSUADE ANYONE!

"I'm a huge fan of Akash's writing style and the way he can distill quite a complex subject into concise bite-sized points you can take away and convert into action. The book covers many different aspects of persuasion from the way you look to the words you use."
~ Rob Cubbon, author of "From Freelancer to Entrepreneur"

Grab the book here:
www.AkashKaria.com/Persuasion

ANTI NEGATIVITY: HOW TO STOP NEGATIVE THINKING AND LEAD A POSITIVE LIFE

"Akash is a master at taking complex ideas and communicating with simplicity and brilliance. He honors your time by presenting what you need to know right away, and follows up with some excellent examples as reinforcement. If you're looking for some simple and effective ways to stop thinking negatively and a new season of positivity, definitely check out this book."
~ Justin Morgan

Grab the book here:
www.AkashKaria.com/AntiNegativity

READY, SET...PROCRASTINATE! 23 ANTI-PROCRASTINATION TOOLS DESIGNED TO HELP YOU STOP PUTTING THINGS OFF AND START GETTING THINGS DONE

"This is one book you should not delay reading! Having struggled with procrastination for much of my life, Akash Karia's book came like a breath of fresh air. He provides clear, practical advice on how to overcome the problem, but warns that you will need to work at it daily. This is a quick, very useful read and with 23 tips on offer, there will be

several that you can identify with and implement for immediate results. If there is just one thing that you should not put off, it is reading this book."
~ Gillian Findlay

Grab the book here:
www.AkashKaria.com/AntiProcrastination

WANT MORE?
Then check out Akash's author-page on Amazon:
www.bit.ly/AkashKaria

ABOUT THE AUTHOR

Akash Karia is an award-winning speaker and peak productivity coach who has been ranked as one of the Top Ten speakers in Asia Pacific. He is an in-demand international speaker who has spoken to a wide range of audiences including bankers in Hong Kong, students in Tanzania, governmental organizations in Dubai and yoga teachers in Thailand. He is regularly sought-out by governments as well as businesses for his expertise on communication, motivation and peak performance psychology.

Akash currently lives in Tanzania where he works as the Chief Commercial Officer of a multi-million dollar company. When he is not writing or lazing around on a beach with a good book in his hands, he is available for speaking engagements and can be contacted through his website: **www.AkashKaria.com**

"Akash is THE best coach I've ever had!"
Eric Laughton, *Certified John Maxwell Trainer, United States*

"If you want to learn presentation skills, public speaking or just simply uncover excellence hidden inside of you or your teams, Akash Karia is the coach to go to."
Raju Mandhyan, *TV show host, Expat Insights, Philippines*

Voted as one of the "10 online entrepreneurs you need to know in 2015"
The Expressive Leader

Featured as one of the "top 9 [online] presentations of 2014"
AuthorStream.com

"Akash is a phenomenal coach! The information I gained in just a few short hours is priceless."
Fatema Dewji, *Director of Marketing for billion-dollar conglomerate, MeTL, Tanzania*

"I loved the two days with Akash, which were filled with useful information. His passion and enthusiasm made the classes fun and exciting."
Pricilla Alberd, *Australia*

"The two days in Akash's workshop have been excellent, very informative and packed with knowledge...tons of practical, ready to use techniques."
Edyte Peszlo, *Sales and Procurement Manager, Thailand*

"I found the course content very relatable and explained in a way that way not only very easy to understand but also incredibly interesting."
Hayley Mikkos-Martin, *Australia*

"Akash Karia is a fine public speaker who knows his subject very well. A rare talent who has much in store for you as an individual, and better yet, your organization."
Sherilyn Pang, *Business Reporter, Capital TV, Malaysia*

Grab your Free Success Toolkit:
www.AkashKaria.com/Free

Check out more Great books:
www.bit.ly/AkashKaria

Email for Speaking-related Inquires:
akash@akashkaria.com / akash.speaker@gmail.com

Connect on LinkedIn:
www.LinkedIn.com/In/AkashKaria

Made in the USA
Coppell, TX
17 November 2021